Tiptoe Into Scary Places

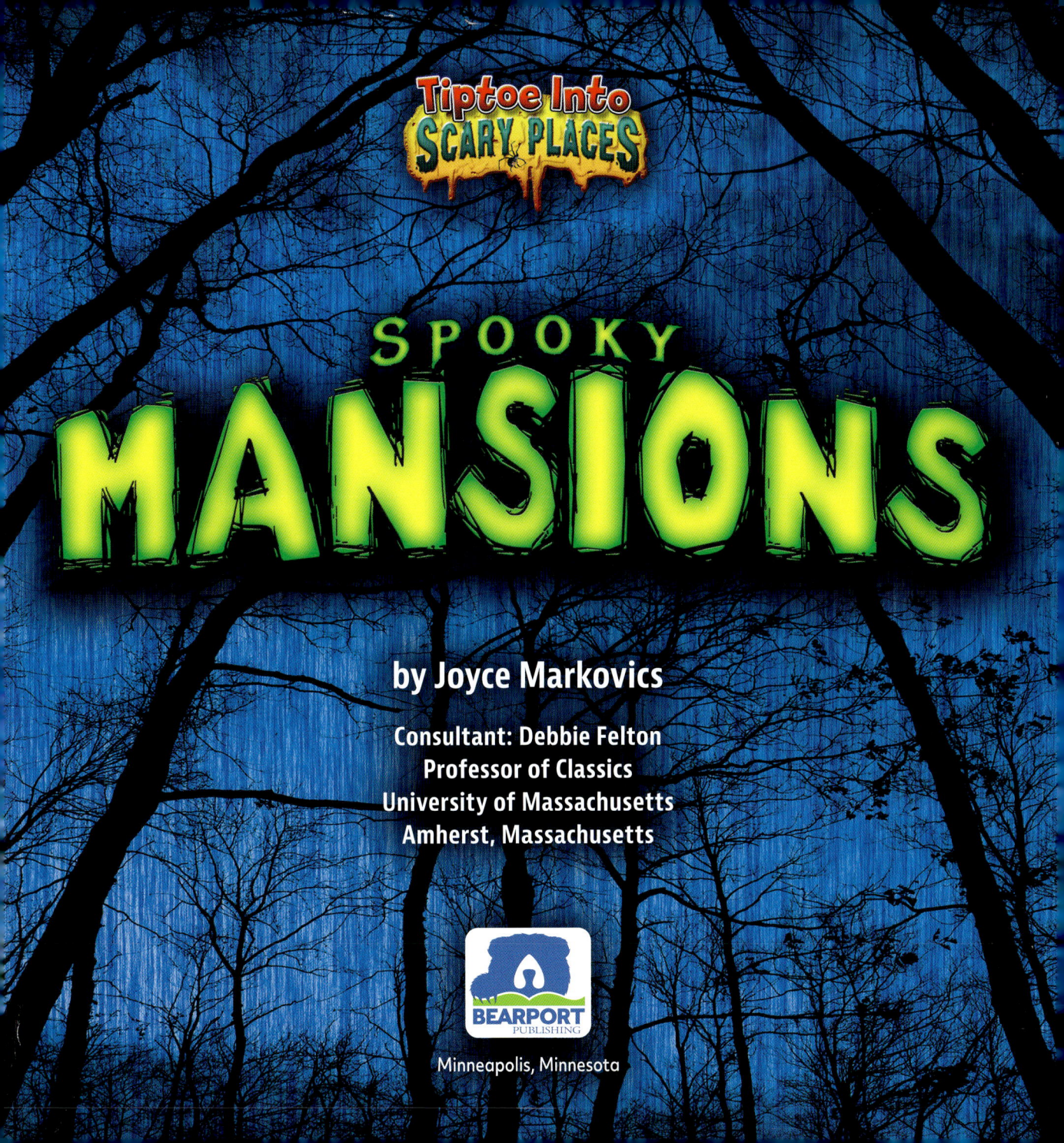

SPOOKY MANSIONS

by Joyce Markovics

Consultant: Debbie Felton
Professor of Classics
University of Massachusetts
Amherst, Massachusetts

BEARPORT
PUBLISHING

Minneapolis, Minnesota

Credits

Cover, © Kim Jones and ©Nikolai Tsvetkov/Shutterstock; 3, Mr Dmitry/Shutterstock; 4–5, © Kim Jones, ©Ysbrand Cosijn/Shutterstock.com, and ©Eric Isselee/Shutterstock.com; 7, © J.W. Ocker; 8, © J.W. Ocker; 9, © J.W. Ocker; 10, William Downie/Wikimedia Commons/Public Domain; 11, © poemnist/Shutterstock; 12, © Lario Tus/Shutterstock; 13, © Shaun Cunningham/Alamy; 14, © Korionov/Shutterstock; 15, © Derek Heidelberg/Wikimedia Commons; 16, © kimberrywood/Shutterstock; 17, © Gina Kelly/Alamy; 18, Public Domain; 19, © thisisbossi/Wikimedia Commons; 20, © Creatus/Shutterstock; 21, © thisisbossi/Wikimedia Commons; 23, © Kris Mari/Shutterstock; and 24, © 12photography/Shutterstock.

President: Jen Jenson
Director of Product Development: Spencer Brinker
Editor: Allison Juda
Designer: Micah Edel
Cover: Kim Jones

Library of Congress Cataloging-in-Publication Data

Names: Markovics, Joyce L., author.
Title: Spooky mansions / by Joyce Markovics.
Description: Minneapolis, Minnesota : Bearport Publishing Company, [2021] | Series: Tiptoe into scary places | Includes bibliographical references and index.
Identifiers: LCCN 2020002394 (print) | LCCN 2020002395 (ebook) | ISBN 9781647471774 (library binding) | ISBN 9781647471835 (ebook)
Subjects: LCSH: Haunted palaces—Juvenile literature. | Ghosts—Juvenile literature.
Classification: LCC BF1474 .M36 2021 (print) | LCC BF1474 (ebook) | DDC 133.1/22—dc23
LC record available at https://lccn.loc.gov/2020002394
LC ebook record available at https://lccn.loc.gov/2020002395

Copyright © 2021 Bearport Publishing Company. All rights reserved. No part of this publication may be reproduced in whole or in part, stored in any retrieval system, or transmitted in any form or by any means, electronic, mechanical, photocopying, recording, or otherwise, without written permission from the publisher.

For more information, write to Bearport Publishing, 5357 Penn Avenue South, Minneapolis, MN 55419. Printed in the United States of America.

CONTENTS

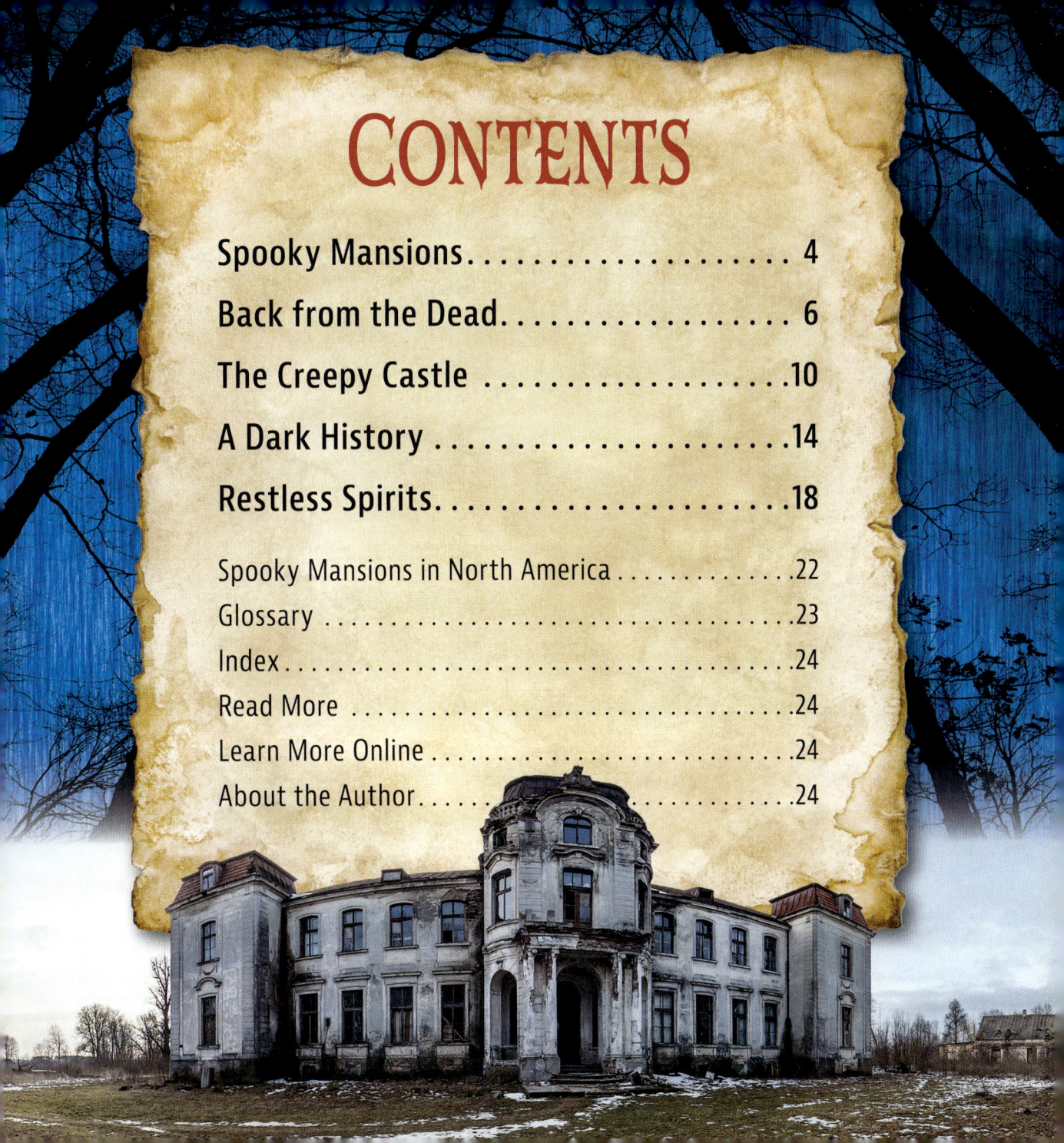

Spooky Mansions 4

Back from the Dead 6

The Creepy Castle .10

A Dark History 14

Restless Spirits 18

Spooky Mansions in North America 22
Glossary 23
Index 24
Read More 24
Learn More Online 24
About the Author 24

Spooky Mansions

A huge, empty house sits high on a hill. One of the windows glows an **eerie** green. The light brightens and then flickers. Suddenly, a thin, hunched figure appears in the window. "Leave my house!" it growls.

Get ready to read four hair-raising stories about spooky mansions. Turn the page . . . if you dare.

Back from the Dead

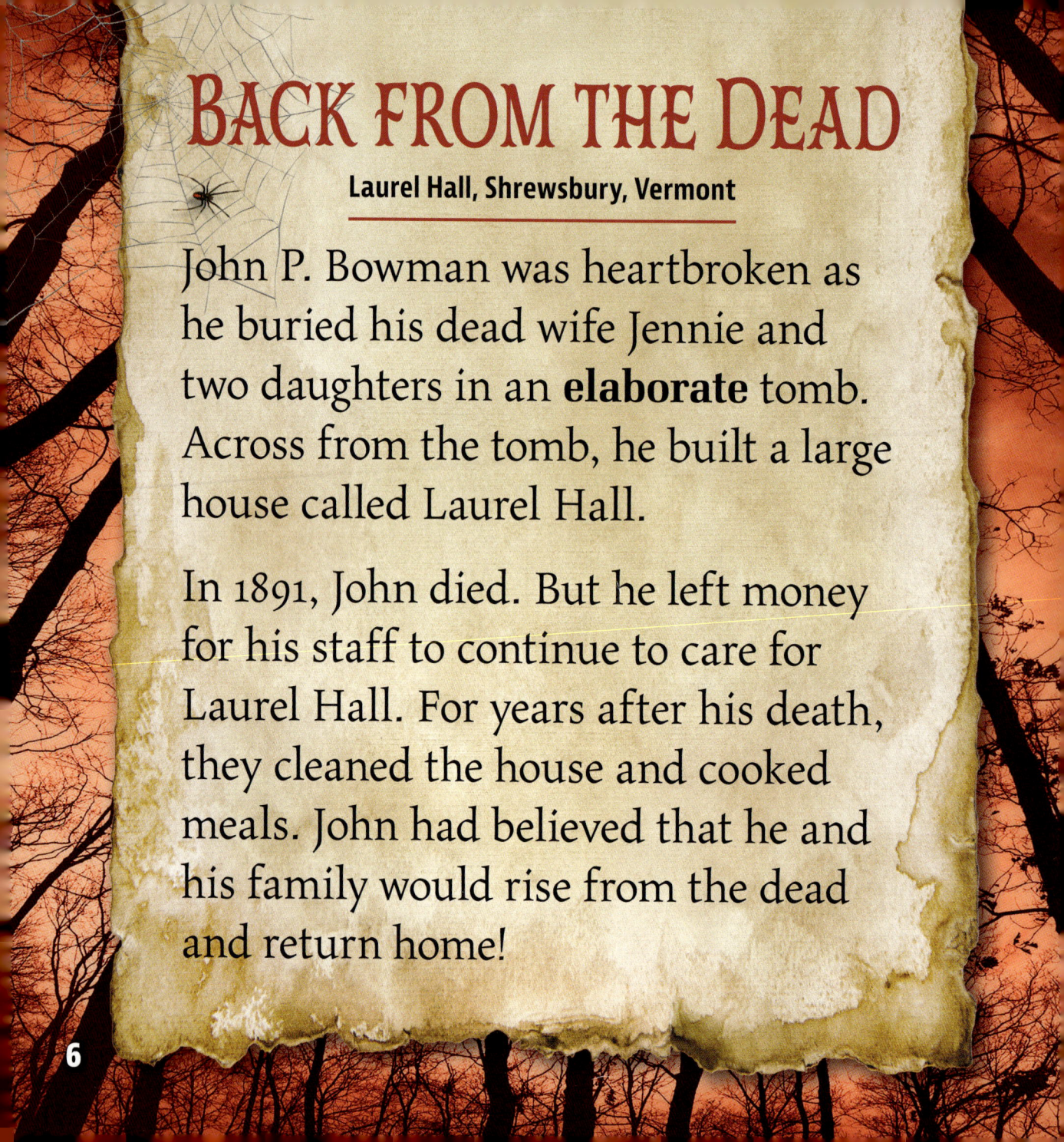

Laurel Hall, Shrewsbury, Vermont

John P. Bowman was heartbroken as he buried his dead wife Jennie and two daughters in an **elaborate** tomb. Across from the tomb, he built a large house called Laurel Hall.

In 1891, John died. But he left money for his staff to continue to care for Laurel Hall. For years after his death, they cleaned the house and cooked meals. John had believed that he and his family would rise from the dead and return home!

Laurel Hall

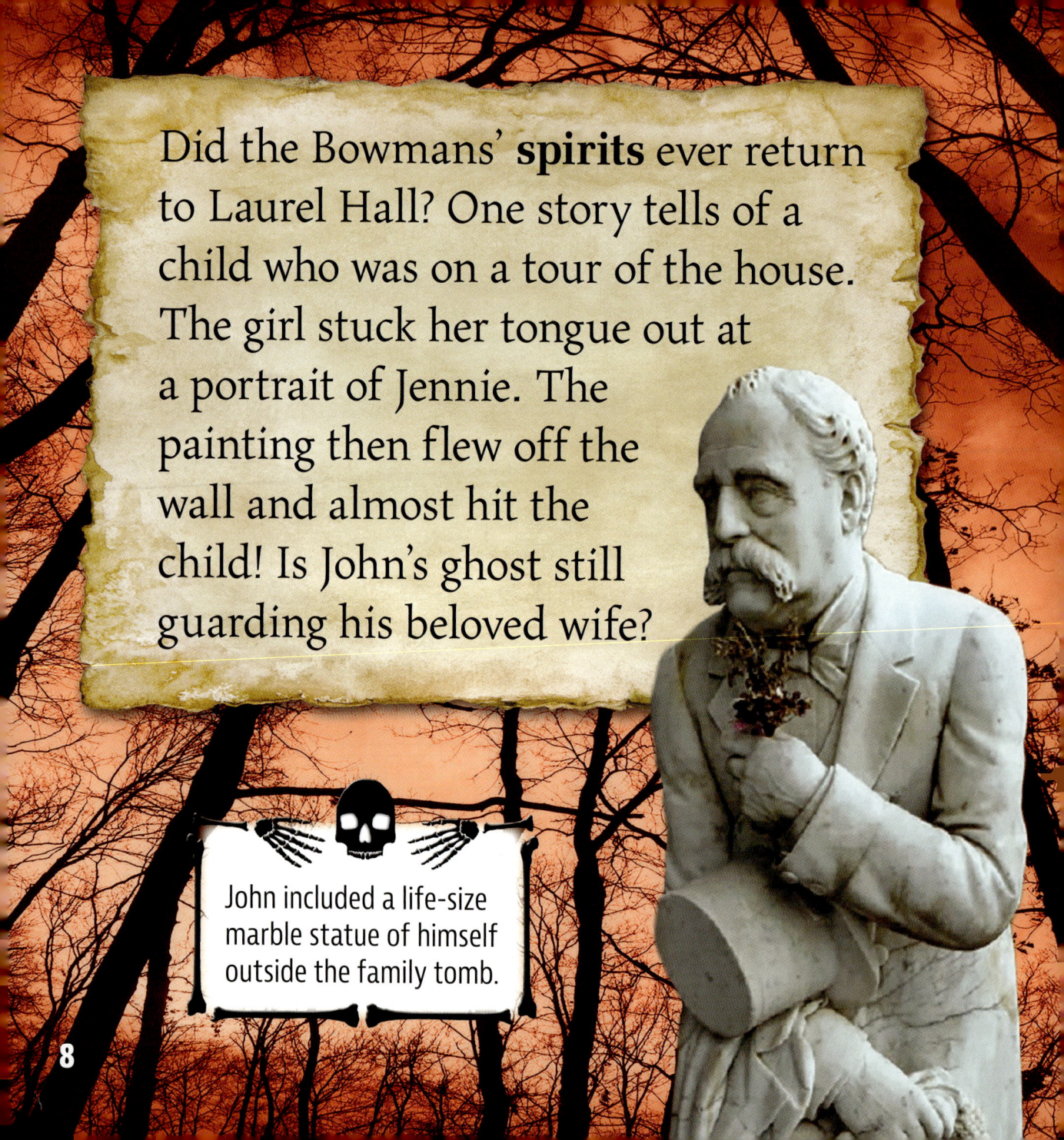

Did the Bowmans' **spirits** ever return to Laurel Hall? One story tells of a child who was on a tour of the house. The girl stuck her tongue out at a portrait of Jennie. The painting then flew off the wall and almost hit the child! Is John's ghost still guarding his beloved wife?

John included a life-size marble statue of himself outside the family tomb.

The Creepy Castle

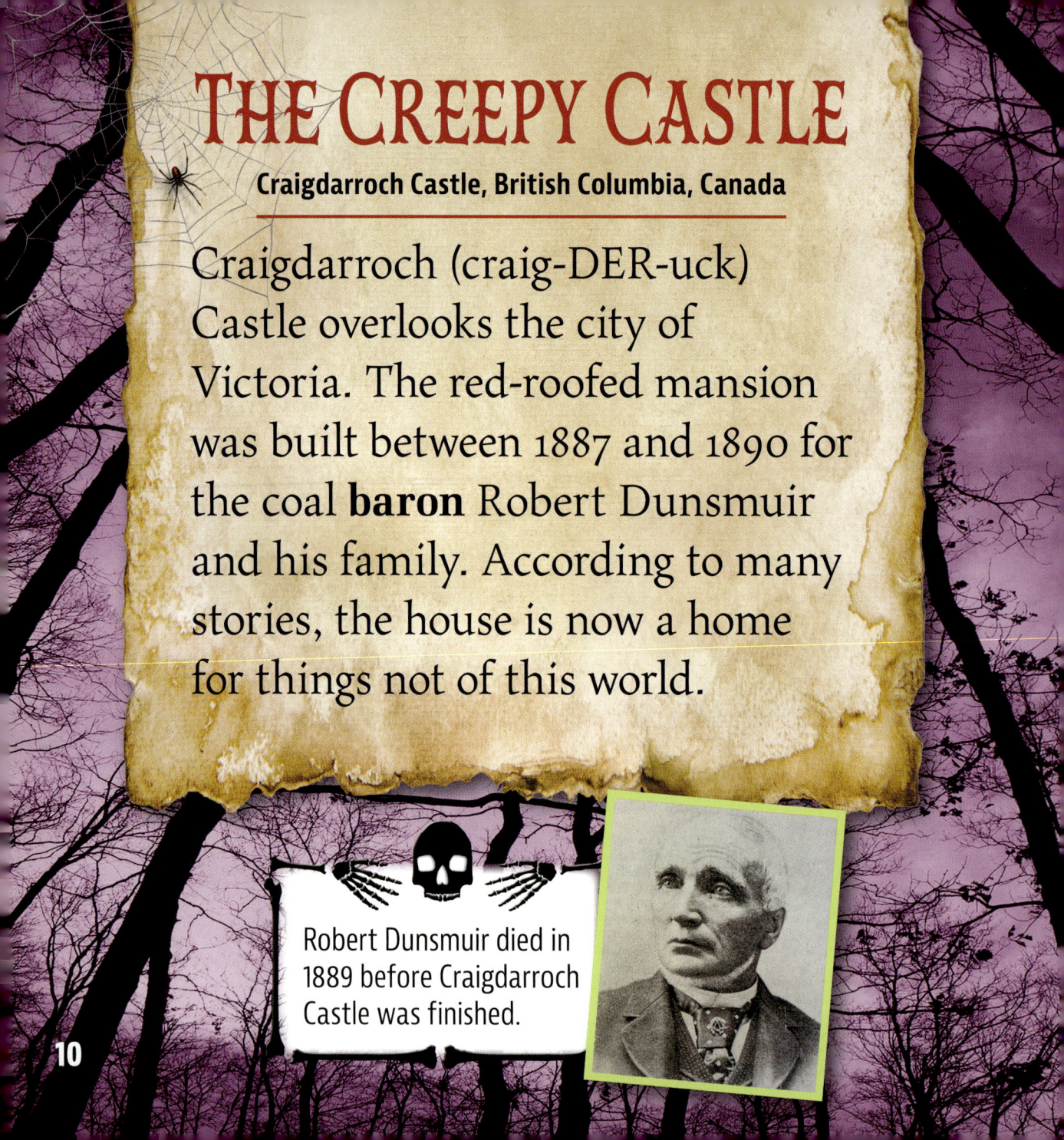

Craigdarroch Castle, British Columbia, Canada

Craigdarroch (craig-DER-uck) Castle overlooks the city of Victoria. The red-roofed mansion was built between 1887 and 1890 for the coal **baron** Robert Dunsmuir and his family. According to many stories, the house is now a home for things not of this world.

Robert Dunsmuir died in 1889 before Craigdarroch Castle was finished.

Craigdarroch Castle

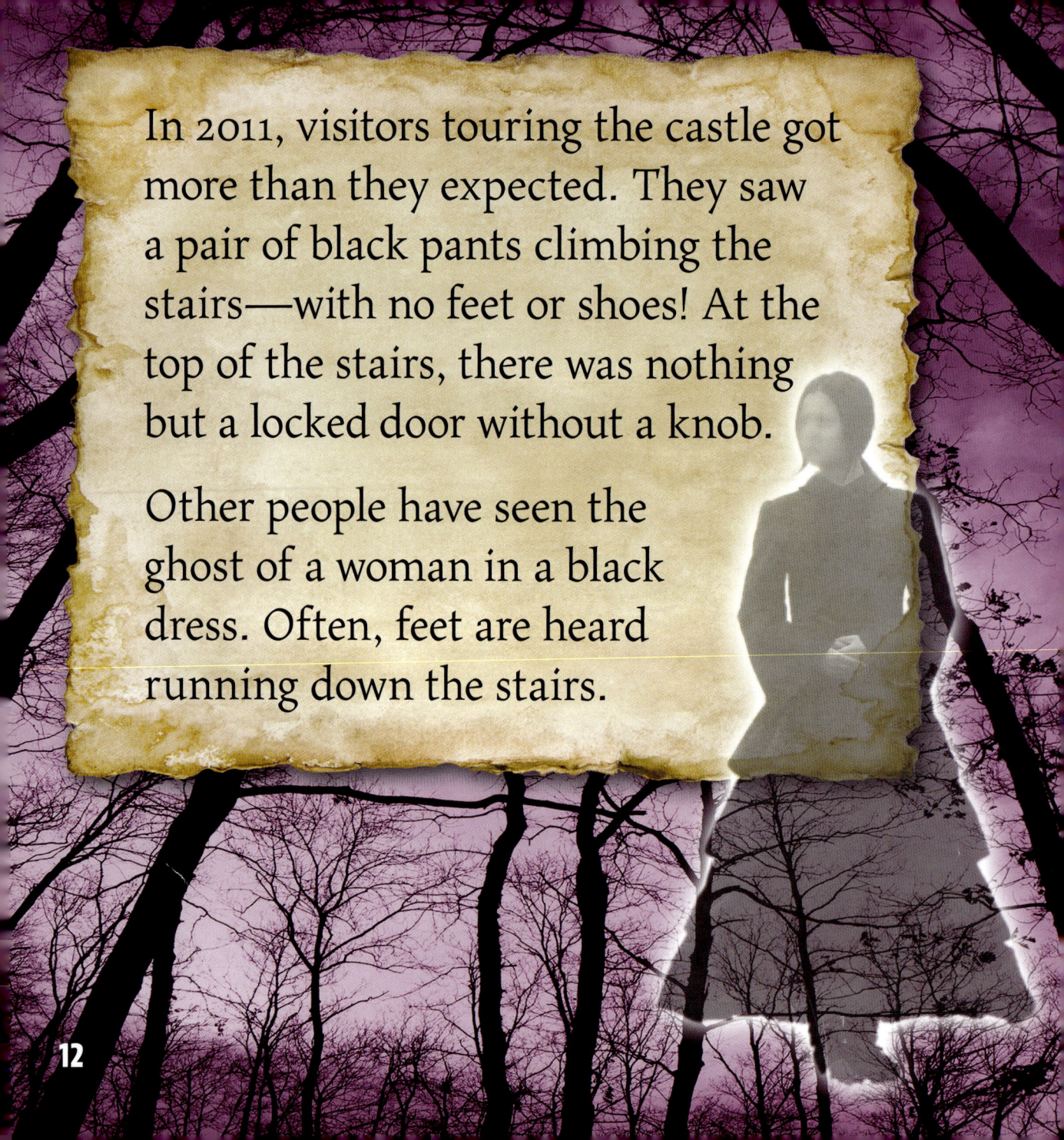

In 2011, visitors touring the castle got more than they expected. They saw a pair of black pants climbing the stairs—with no feet or shoes! At the top of the stairs, there was nothing but a locked door without a knob.

Other people have seen the ghost of a woman in a black dress. Often, feet are heard running down the stairs.

A Dark History

Glensheen Mansion, Duluth, Minnesota

This mansion is as spooky as it is beautiful. On June 27, 1977, two elderly women were found dead inside the grand house.

A man was sent to jail after confessing to the crime. But years later, he changed his story. He said he was not the murderer.

Glensheen mansion was built in 1905. The grand brick house has 39 rooms.

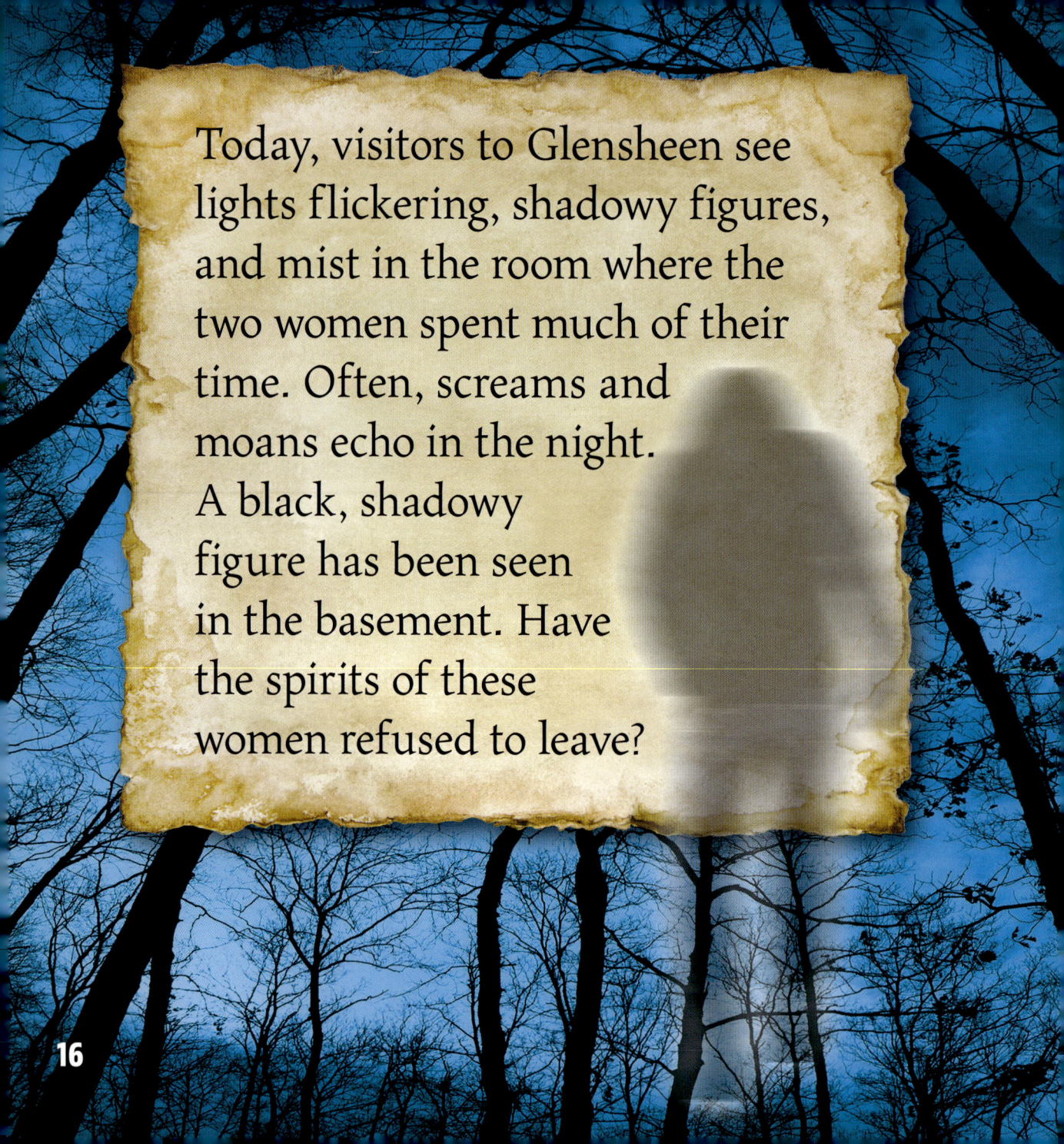

Today, visitors to Glensheen see lights flickering, shadowy figures, and mist in the room where the two women spent much of their time. Often, screams and moans echo in the night. A black, shadowy figure has been seen in the basement. Have the spirits of these women refused to leave?

A room inside Gleensheen Mansion

Restless Spirits

Baker Mansion, Altoona, Pennsylvania

Ghosts lie in wait behind this home's stunning **exterior** . . . lots of them. Elias Baker built the mansion for his family in the 1840s. His wife and children lived there even after his death in 1864. In 1914, the last Baker family member passed away. But, it seems, their spirits still remain in the house.

Elias Baker

Baker Mansion

One summer night, a tour guide was shocked to find the shutters she had just closed wide open. Another time, the **imprint** of a body appeared on a couch in the **parlor**. Suddenly, the room turned icy cold. Many people think the Baker ghosts are to blame.

Another worker heard a cane tapping on the floor in the empty house. It was believed to be the ghost of Elias Baker, who walked with a cane.

Spooky Mansions in North America

Craigdarroch Castle
British Columbia, Canada

This old mansion is filled with stairs—and a footless spirit.

Glensheen Mansion
Duluth, Minnesota

Check out this beautiful house with a dark past.

Laurel Hall
Shrewsbury, Vermont

Learn about John P. Bowman's home and the spirits that share it.

Baker Mansion
Altoona, Pennsylvania

Explore a mansion and its many ghosts.

22

Glossary

baron (BA-ruhn) a powerful person in a certain business

eerie (IHR-ee) mysterious or strange

elaborate (i-LAB-ur-it) marked by a lot of detail

exterior (ek-STIHR-ee-ur) the outside

imprint (IM-print) a mark made by pressure

parlor (PAHR-ler) a living room

spirits (SPIHR-its) ghosts

Index

Baker, Elias 18, 20
Baker Mansion 18–19, 21–22
Bowman, John P. 6, 8, 22
Craigdarroch Castle 10–13, 22
Dunsmuir, Robert 10
Glensheen Mansion 14–17, 22
Laurel Hall 6–8, 22
tomb 6, 8

Read More

Rudolph, Jessica. *Creaky Castles (Tiptoe Into Scary Places).* New York: Bearport (2017).

Rudolph, Jessica. *Ghost Houses (Tiptoe Into Scary Places).* New York: Bearport (2017).

Learn More Online

1. Go to **www.factsurfer.com**
2. Enter "**Spooky Mansions**" into the search box.
3. Click on the cover of this book to see a list of websites.

About the Author

Joyce Markovics has written over 100 books for children. She loves old, spooky places and volunteers as a gravestone cleaner in Ossining, New York.